Paranormal Crimes

Supernatural and Unexplained True Crime Cases that Have Mystified Authorities

Conrad Bauer

Contents

Introduction
Close Encounters of the Criminal Kind

The idea of being confronted with a paranormal phenomenon of any kind is enough to flabbergast most people. But what if that paranormal phenomenon is coupled with a crime? Seeing a Bigfoot in the wilderness would be stunning enough, but imagine one grabbing your wallet and running off with it! The same goes for folks who claim to have been attacked by ghosts, demons and the like. There are even some who say they somehow got on the bad side of elves, fairies or other woodland sprites. And while everyday crooks are bad enough, when an entity that can walk through walls and travel through space and time starts giving you the shakedown, it adds a whole new dimension to the matter—literally!

The stories herein are admittedly hard to believe all the way around, but those telling them, seem sincere enough. So, whether you believe them or not, suspend your judgment for a moment as we take a look at some of the most astonishing alleged close encounters—of the criminal kind!

Sequestered by Sasquatch

When it comes to cases of paranormal abduction, most people probably think of little grey-skinned aliens. But these are not the only paranormal entities that stand accused of kidnapping. The hairy, apelike creature known as Bigfoot has also generated its fair share of abduction stories.

Take the case of Jason Richardson. Jason was a middle-aged outdoorsman who was out hiking one afternoon in Northern California. The hike was supposed to take him from Lake Tahoe to the summit of Mount Tallac and back, a strenuous journey of around ten miles. His bizarre encounter began some time before he reached the peak when he heard a "guttural" yet simultaneously "babyish" voice whining in the distance as he stopped to take a drink. Worried that a baby had been abandoned in the wilderness, he immediately put his water bottle back in his pack and headed toward the sound. But he didn't make it very far, because out of nowhere, something struck him from behind and he went out like a light.

He regained consciousness several hours later, disoriented and unsure of where he was. He seemed to be inside a cave, and he could hear running water in the background, but other than that he was at a complete loss. Shortly afterward, he came to the startling realization that he was not alone.

He looked up to see "two bear-like creatures" who seemed to be vigorously debating what to do with him in the "same guttural tone of voice" that he had heard from the trail. The creatures' torsos and legs "were covered in thick red hair." The first thing that came to mind was that they were a pair of bears walking upright. At the same time, though, he knew that they were not really bears; they were creatures of a whole other magnitude. That much was evident from their communication with each other. They were obviously intelligent—more intelligent than any known bears, at least. They also knew how to restrain their prey, which Jason quickly discovered when he realized that his ankles and hands had been tied together by vines. He was quite understandably in a state of shock, but he was able to notice the basic details about them. Strangely, even though the beings as a whole were very hairy, their necks were absolutely hairless. Their heads were covered with red hair and black feathers.

Jason decided against speaking to these bizarre creatures, reasoning that it could just anger them and make an obviously bad situation even worse. Instead, he just tried to go with the flow and hope for the best. But as much as he tried to keep a lower profile, it wasn't long before one of the Bigfoots walked over and gave him a swift kick to the sternum. Jason, predictably enough, cried out in pain. This seemed to please the Bigfoot, but not necessarily out of sadism; it seemed more like the creature was just happy to see that Jason was still alive after he had been staying still and quiet as a statue. The next thing he knew, the Bigfoots brought out a variety of stone and wooden tools and used them to cut through the vines that bound him.

Although free, Jason initially maintained the low profile he'd decided was his best course of action. He made no attempt to communicate with his captors or to escape. Instead, he simply leaned against the wall contemplating the strange predicament he was in. Maybe the Bigfoots didn't find his glum disposition very entertaining, or maybe they'd simply gotten tired of having him around, but after a while, they apparently decided to get rid of him. One of the creatures approached him without a word (or even a grunt), grabbed him by the arms and legs, and unceremoniously tossed him out of the cave. To emphasize the point, the other one then hurled a large rock that just missed Jason's head.

Jason could take a hint; he knew that his time was up and his erstwhile hosts were telling him to hit the road. He hightailed it back to the trail and started hiking back to his car as fast as he could. It was only when he reached it that he bothered to check his watch and learned that his ordeal had lasted for over 10 hours. Whether or not the pesky Bigfeet who nabbed him and confined him against his will realized that their actions were criminal, it was certainly an ordeal that Jason Richardson would never forget.

Attacked by Apparitions

In 2012 a woman named Karen moved her family into her dream home in Baltimore, Maryland. The dream quickly turned into a nightmare, which sounds like the beginning of any number of campfire ghost stories—but this incident is taken from the pages of real life.

Karen didn't know it, because the real estate agent had somehow left this fact out of the listing, but her new home was the scene of a grisly murder-suicide involving its previous occupants. She found out the truth one day when she was gardening and a neighborhood boy approached and asked her a rather odd question. In a completely innocent manner, the child inquired, "Did you guys see any blood in there?"

Beyond puzzled, Karen stammered, "What? Blood? What on Earth are you talking about?"

After several weeks of smiling neighbors and cursory introductions, this little boy then dropped the bombshell that no one else had wanted to. He explained that the husband and wife who used to live in the house had frequently engaged in loud arguments. It was an incessant noise that everyone heard but no one knew what to do about. The police had been called anonymously on a couple of occasions, but since there were no signs of violence, they had simply told the squabbling couple to tone it down. So the arguing continued, for years, until it became just another part of everyday life in the neighborhood, something people tuned out just as easily as their neighbors' lawnmowers and leaf blowers.

That is until it stopped. In the end, ironically, it was the sudden, solemn silence that spurred the neighbors to act. When they noticed that the house had been quiet for a few days they got worried and called the police. This time, the responding officers didn't find hotheaded husband and wife screaming at each other. They found a trail of blood leading to the kitchen—and to the corpses of the couple, dead from a murder-suicide.

It's amazing how knowledge can open doors. And when Karen's family learned the history of their house, some kind of door certainly flew open. Whether it was a door of perception that allowed them to imagine strange happenings, or a door directly to the spirit realm that allowed ghosts to come through and attack, the uncanny phenomena began almost as soon as the little boy left.

The first thing the family noticed was items falling off the walls for no apparent reason—and ominously enough, these items more often than not had some sort of religious character.

Paintings of angels fell to the floor, crucifixes flew off the wall, and a tapestry depicting the Last Supper came sliding down. The family also began to see other typical indications of ghostly activity, such as doors and cabinets opening and shutting at random. Soon enough they were also hearing a low, deep voice, nearly inaudible but murmuring just loudly enough to be heard in between all the slamming doors and crashing religious icons.

Even more disturbingly, the male voice was sometimes accompanied by a female voice crying out in fear and pain. Knowing what they now knew, Karen's family were sure that they were hearing the spirits of the former residents reenacting a grisly murder-suicide in front of their ears. This is hardly uncommon; the spirits of people who meet violent ends often seem stuck in the moment of the trauma, and many hauntings are essentially spiritual feedback loops that simply repeat horrific experiences over and over.

But as Karen's family would quickly find out, these spirits were not just reliving their bloodcurdling past—they were also able and eager to interact with the present. This was first demonstrated when the male apparition began calling out to Karen's teenage daughter by name, whispering, "Anne! Anne!" over and over. But while mother and daughter were being tormented by these unseen forces, Karen's son David was none the wiser. In fact, he became angry whenever his mother and sister mentioned their suspicions that the home was haunted. Call it a spiritual blind spot or a spiritual shield, but David seemed to be able to block the whole thing out. And as the attacks on the two women escalated, David definitely began to look like the lucky one.

The malevolent force soon turned on Karen, launching a vicious assault when she was at her most vulnerable—in bed, sound asleep. Karen was jolted from her slumber in the middle of the night by the sound of someone crawling up the stairs just outside her bedroom. At first, she thought that her children must be playing a joke on her, so as any mother would, she yelled, "Guys knock it off!" But what she heard next made her realize that she was not scolding her children—she was reprimanding a ghost! Because her sleepy command to "knock it off" was met with deep-throated evil laughter followed by a booming voice shouting, "No!"

Hot on the heels of this guttural, unearthly refusal, the evil entity flew up the stairs and right into Karen's room. She clearly saw its shadowy form standing at the foot of her bed. Almost paralyzed with fear, she tried to hide under the covers, but the black shadow formed dark skeletal hands and used one of them to rip the cover off... and the next thing Karen knew, she was waking up with the sun streaming through the window. Reassured that the whole thing had just been a nightmare, she got up and went to brush her hair—but upon looking in the mirror, she saw what appeared to be strangulation marks around her neck! Was it a dream? Or an attack by an evil apparition? To this day, Karen can't say for sure—but she slept with the hallway light on for several years thereafter.

Another case of assault by apparition is interesting not so much because of the apparition itself but because of the influence the apparition exerted on its subject. Ghost hunter Robert Laursen was investigating a haunted house in Iowa where an ax-wielding lunatic had murdered the entire household in 1912. The scene of the infamous Villisca axe murders may not sound like a prime tourist spot, but as a professional ghost hunter, Robert saw it as a potential treasure trove of information. So he loaded up with all of his paranormal gear—tape recorders, magnetometers and the like—and hunkered down for an overnight stay. He reckoned he was ready for just about anything that might take place.

So, what happened? He fell asleep and woke up in the morning to find that he had stabbed himself! The wound was so severe that he had to be airlifted to a level I trauma center. Just how does one stab himself nearly to death in his sleep? By the influence of an evil spirit, of course! Whether apparitions directly attack an individual or cause someone to harm himself, the results can be rather dire.

Exterminated by Extraterrestrials

Aliens, ETs, extraterrestrials—whatever you want to call them, they are one of the most popular facets of what we commonly refer to as the paranormal. But for those of us who haven't actually encountered one of these entities ourselves, most of what we believe about them probably has more to do with Hollywood than the facts. And specifically, with Steven Spielberg, whose smash hit *Close Encounters of the Third Kind*

was the first film to feature the little grey aliens we've all come to know and love—and who then made an even bigger blockbuster called *ET*, in which a loveable little alien tries to phone home.

The truth, though, is that most actual accounts of encounters with the occupants of UFOs don't have them acting anywhere near as friendly as they did with Elliott in *ET*. Just consider the cattle mutilations that have left perfectly good cuts of beef scattered all over the countryside. ETs have been implicated in this phenomenon for several reasons. For one thing, it's common that the soft tissues—including the tongue, anus, and genitals—are completely "cored out" while the muscle tissue is left intact. Terrestrial predators and poachers alike would much prefer to eat the meat and leave the soft organs for the vultures, so it's a little implausible to blame the mutilations on carnivores or cattle rustlers. Furthermore, testing on the carcasses has all but proven that they were butchered by surgical lasers. And if the ETs are indeed responsible, they're some pretty sick space travelers, because necropsies have shown that some of these cows were still alive while they were being sliced open.

Not all of the evidence comes from postmortems, either; more than one eyewitness has come forward to implicate the aliens. One man allegedly saw a hovering UFO pick up one of his cows as it grazed. Still munching its last mouthful of grass, the poor beast was lifted high into the air by some sort of tractor beam before a pinpoint laser shot out from underneath the spacecraft and began a grisly mutilation process in which the animal was taken apart piece by piece in a horrific vivisection.

And it isn't just cattle that have allegedly suffered from such crimes. They're not nearly as well-known as the cattle mutilations, but shockingly enough there are reported cases of *human* mutilation as well. Many of them have occurred in war zones, which ETs, for whatever reason, seem to enjoy visiting.

Accounts of UFOs (and sometimes their alien occupants) dropping in on pitched battles date back at least to World War II. It's been hypothesized that ET scientists are interested in studying human warfare—but if some of the stories are true, that's not all they're interested in. Some of them have allegedly been seen picking up wounded servicemen—not to interview them, but to dissect them!

One of these incidents was witnessed by a whole battalion of American soldiers deep in the jungles of Vietnam. They were walking through the wilderness when they came upon a clearing—and sitting right in the middle of it was what looked an awful lot like an alien spacecraft out of a science fiction movie. It was saucer-shaped, "highly reflective" and had highly advanced machinery whirring frenetically all over its surface. Engaged in equally frenzied activity on the ground around the UFO was a group of extraterrestrials of the classic grey alien type.

Already shocked almost out of their wits, the soldiers got an even bigger shock when they realized what the beings were up to: They were busy chucking human corpses and body parts into some kind of high-tech storage containers as if they were scavenging a biological junkyard for human parts. It didn't look like they'd killed the men; apparently, they had come upon the aftermath of a battle and decided not to let the dead bodies go to waste. Still, desecration of a corpse is a criminal offense not matter what star system you may be from, and when the soldiers saw their deceased comrades in arms being treated in this manner, their shock turned to rage.

With his battalion still hidden in the surrounding brush, the American commander audaciously gave the order to open fire on the extraterrestrial grave robbers. The creatures seemed to be wearing some pretty impressive body armor, though; although a few of them were killed by shots to their heads, most of the bullets in the initial barrage bounced right off of them. The response was swift, with the aliens—or possibly autonomous AI weapons systems on their ship—firing beam weapons that burned through (and in some cases practically disintegrated)) any soldier they hit.

Realizing that his troops were severely outgunned, the commander ordered them to retreat back into the woods. The ETs, who apparently weren't really looking for a fight with the living, did not pursue them. Instead, they quickly finished loading the containers of human body parts onto their ship and got the hell out of Dodge in style: The UFO lit up like a Christmas tree, shot straight up into the sky, and rocketed off to parts unknown.

The soldiers who were there would later recall—both in conversation and in recurring nightmares—that the aliens were gathering body parts from both American and North Vietnamese troops. Still, the question remains: Were these ETs relatively harmless scavengers collecting the crumbs of battle—or had they stepped into the battle and killed and mutilated everyone on both sides? When you're dealing with cosmic criminal opportunists like these, who really knows?

Aliens are accused of quite a bit in UFO lore, but dissecting living people isn't usually part of their modus operandi. *Usually...* but then there's this tale of one of the most disturbing alien encounters ever.

It occurred in 1946, a full year before the UFO phenomenon even hit the headlines, in a small Brazilian village. A man named Filho was walking home from work when he got a distinct feeling that he was being watched. He got back to his house without incident, but he couldn't shrug the strange sensation off. He told his family about it, and while they weren't sure what to make of it, they could see that it had made the normally unflappable Filho awfully afraid. They started to get worried too.

Their fears were justified in horrific fashion just a couple of hours later when Filho, standing in the living room, looked out the open window and saw something hovering in the distance, just above the treetops. As he stared at it curiously, the other members of the family saw a blinding white light flash through the window and zap him like a bolt of lightning. The object in the sky then took off rapidly, leaving a stunned Filho lying on the floor.

He was in surprisingly good shape at first, although he mentioned that his skin felt warm as if he had a fever. But this fever quickly went from uncomfortable to unbearable as his skin grew hotter and hotter. Soon he was screaming in pain because he felt like his whole body was on fire as if he were baking from the inside out. His family had no idea what do to, and eventually, the agonized Filho burst out of the house and began yelling to the neighbors for help. One of them offered to give him a ride to the hospital, but he was a gruesome sight by the time he got there. His body was decomposing, with large chunks of flesh dissolving from the unexplainable heat. Filho was melting like an ice cream cone, and in the end, he perished right there in the hospital bed while the physicians stood by, horrified and unable to do anything about it.

While Filho was not exactly mutilated, he was definitely subjected to something highly unusual, whether a weapon or some lethal medical experiment. A more classic case of human mutilation also occurred in Brazil, near Guarapiranga, where the corpse of a local man was found sprawled on its back with the eyes, tongue, stomach, and genitals completely removed. Even more disturbing, the autopsy showed that all this had been done while the man was still alive. He had died of pain, shock, and fear as his organs were ripped out with great precision, apparently using the same sort of high-tech surgical equipment identified in the cattle mutilations. Photos of his corpse show empty eye sockets staring out blankly—and a tongue-less mouth fixed in a silent scream.

A more recent case occurred in the early 2000s in the remote Indian village of Shawna. Townspeople were allegedly attacked several times by a "soccer ball with sparkling lights"—something like an extraterrestrial drone—that would fly through the village and blast intense heat rays at random inhabitants. Many people were hurt, and one man, Ramji Pal, was burned so badly that he later died. Now, these attacks happened during the summer, when most people in Shawna slept with their windows open (or even outdoors). This has led some skeptics to assert that the villagers most likely fell victim to parasitic insects, bats or some other wild animal—not aliens. But the idea that Ramji Pal died of bug bites doesn't sit too well with his friends and family. They say they know full well what happened to him, and they insist that something otherworldly did indeed arrive to attack him in the middle of the night. According to them, no bugs could have inflicted anything like the grievous wounds he suffered. Like so many other witnesses to paranormal crimes, they know what they saw, and no one else can convince them otherwise.

Choked by a Chupacabra

Even among paranormal criminals, the chupacabra is a strange creature. The name, meaning "goat-sucker", is Spanish, reflecting the fact that the chupacabra first came to prominence in rural regions of Latin America—including Puerto Rico, El Salvador, Honduras, and Mexico—in the early 1990s. Since then it's moved northward and now sometimes surfaces in southern U.S. states such as Florida and Texas.

So what does this paranormal perp want? Supposedly blood from barnyard animals—and if it can't get that, blood from human beings! In fact, the incident that sent investigators rushing to Puerto Rico and cemented the chupacabra's fame back in the 90s involved two American tourists who had been discovered by local farmers with their "throats torn out" and completely "drained of blood". A horrific fate, to be sure, but is there any proof that the chupacabra was the culprit? That's precisely what an intrepid pair of paranormal investigators set out to discover.

They went around the Puerto Rican countryside interviewing everyone who might know something, from civil defense officials and cops on the beat to cattlemen and farmhands. The farmers were the ones on the front lines, and many gave horrendous reports of waking up in the morning to find their chickens lying dead inside their coops, completely drained of blood. Just like in the cattle mutilations, the meatiest part of the bird—in fact, *all* of the bird—was left intact, so it was clear that this was not the work of any known carnivore (which probably couldn't have gotten into the coops anyway). And if the farmers had a chicken thief on their hands, it was a chicken thief who was only interested in stealing the birds' blood!

A short time after the investigators reported their findings, famed Canadian filmmaker Paul Kimball and his camera crew traveled to Puerto Rico to scope out the mysterious depths of the El Yunque rainforest. In a nearby village, they met a man named

Pucho who claimed to have encountered the chupacabra in person while he was walking to services at the Church of the Three Kings. But the first thing he heard on this particular Sunday morning wasn't a sermon; it was a "loud roar" from the woods behind the church, followed by the flapping of wings. The startled Pucho looked up just in time to see a bat-like biped flying out of the forest and on towards a nearby farm.

This farm had plenty of cattle, and plenty of goats, and sure enough, in the days following Pucho's sighting its unfortunate owner found a number of them dead and drained of blood. Other farmers in the area also lost livestock in the same manner. The dead animals all had the same double puncture wounds to the jugular vein, apparently made by a large set of fangs. Aside from the chupacabra, the only possible culprit for these crimes would be a very large vampire bat, and in fact, that's not terribly out of line with Pucho's description. But to suggest that one vampire bat—even a really big one—could have caused so much mayhem on multiple farms is so unlikely as to be completely absurd.

The chupacabra has continued to wreak havoc on Puerto Rico's farms, but it's largely faded from the news over the past decade. After the first few times, it seems, "Chupacabra Sucks Goat" doesn't get any more page views than "Dog Bites Man". Furthermore, some purported evidence for the existence of the chupacabra was debunked in the early 2010s when several supposed chupacabra corpses and skeletons were proven to be nothing more than the remains of disease-ravaged dogs. Indeed, the case has been made that chupacabras, in general, are nothing more than coyotes and other wild canines suffering from a combination of rabies and mange. The mange, which causes most of their fur to fall out, is said to account for their strange appearance, while rabies explains their strange behavior.

On the other hand, any zoologist would tell you that coyotes don't live in Puerto Rico. Pucho would point out that dogs don't have wings. And all those chicken farmers would contend that no vampire bat could have drained the blood from their birds while they were safely locked inside a chicken coop. If ever the suspects are all gathered together, it's the chupacabra they'll be picking out of the lineup.

Raped by a Reptilian

This book focuses on crimes committed by paranormal entities—
but what about crimes committed *against* paranormal entities?
Wait, what? Did someone mug Santa Claus? Did the Easter
Bunny end up as rabbit stew? Just what are we talking about
here? Well, let me tell you. Police in Seattle, Washington,
recently arrested a man who claims to have killed a shapeshifting
reptilian!

Now, if the word "reptilian" just conjures images of snakes and
turtles, be aware that this is actually a recognized paranormal
entity. There are folks around the globe who are totally
convinced that reptile-like humanoids that can change their

appearance at will do indeed live among us. And this is allegedly what Bucky Wolfe believed on the day that police paid him a visit and found his brother with a sword sticking out of his head.

Bucky had told the 911 dispatcher, "God told me he was a lizard!" At the station house, he told detectives that he was schizophrenic and was seeing reptilian "lizard people" everywhere he went. Then he began shouting, "Kill me, kill me, I can't live in this reality!" It turned out that—although he had never been officially diagnosed with any form of mental illness—the 26-year-old Seattle native had been mentally unstable for some time.

He was also an adherent of the conspiracy theory holding that global elites are in fact shapeshifting reptilians. This theory was first popularized by the controversial David Iche in the late 1990s, but opinion is still divided as to the origin of the reptilians. Some true believers say they are extraterrestrials, while others maintain that they are a highly advanced underground Earth civilization unknown to human society. Both schools of thought, however, allege that the reptilians are extremely aggressive. And if they are ETs, the reptilians are apparently much more concupiscent than most. Because whereas the grey aliens are known to do some rather invasive probing with their instruments, the reptilians sometimes stoop to sexual assault of those they abduct.

Niara Terea Isley, a former radar operator for the U.S. Air Force, was one alleged victim. Niara is a woman with good credentials and high security clearance—and also one who tells an unbelievably fantastic story: She claims that these beings took her on multiple excursions to their slave mines on the dark side of the moon. And when she wasn't helping drill into the lunar surface, she was the one getting drilled as she was passed around like a living sex toy for the pleasure of bipedal reptilian creatures. A woman named Giovanna Podda relates a similarly sinister narrative involving reptilian beings. She says that the reptilians brought her aboard a flying saucer, set her down on a metal bed, and proceeded to gang-rape her. Putting a paranormal twist on the #MeToo movement, several others have since come forward with similar stories.

Is this for real? Or is it all just a kinky fantasy? Who can know for sure? Either way, the paranormal crimes that have been alleged are highly disturbing!

Stolen from by Skinwalkers

Known by the Navajo as *yee naaldlooshii*—"he who goes on all fours"—the skinwalker is a staple of Native American lore. They appear out of nowhere, usually when their victims are all alone, and proceed to give them the fright of their life. As the Navajo name implies, a skinwalker is first observed as an animal—typically a coyote, wolf or large dog—before shapeshifting into humanoid form.

Motorists passing through remote stretches of the Southwest have provided many of the modern accounts of skinwalkers. The stories usually begin with the narrator driving along a lonely stretch of road and coming upon a dog-like animal. The creature then begins to chase the car—and unlike an ordinary car-chasing dog, it begins to catch up to the speeding vehicle! The astonished driver accelerates to shake the beast off his tail, but the animal keeps gaining on him even as the speedometer passes 70 miles per hour. It's usually at this point that the unbelievably fast "animal" suddenly transforms into a human or humanoid. The driver looks in the rearview mirror and it's no longer a large dog chasing him but a tall, skinny person! The skinwalker might then saunter up to the motorist's driver side window (as much as anything can saunter at 70 MPH) and simply grin or laugh at him before turning around and running back in the other direction.

As frightening as all this may be, in many cases, this is the extent of it. There's no real harm done; the skinwalker's main goal seems to be simply scaring the crap out of people. Like many paranormal entities, skinwalkers seem to thrive on fear, and some researchers suspect that they literally feed off it. This would explain their dramatic efforts to terrify innocent motorists— they're stirring up negative energy for themselves to feed upon before letting the frightened fish they've caught back into the pond. That's why they make the experience as frightening as possible.

But at the same time, it is said that the less fear you show toward a skinwalker, the less it can do to you. Getting frightened and running away will only encourage it, but if you simply turn and face it down, the skinwalker itself will soon shrink with fear. That's exactly what happened in one account in which a skinwalker threatened a man's little brother. The beast looked like it was about to leap upon the boy, so big brother charged right at it with his arms flailing in the air. The creature, absolutely shocked at the resistance it was facing, abruptly turned and fled the scene of the crime. Just like everyday bullies, the skinwalker seems to crumble at the merest show of strength.

This was also demonstrated in the case of Paul Martinez, who claims that he was confronted by a skinwalker while visiting his girlfriend in New Mexico. The couple drove Paul's pickup truck to a remote stretch of desert and were camped out under the stars when Paul got up to answer a call of nature. He walked over to a nearby bush and began to urinate—and as he was doing so, he felt something brush against his back. Still preoccupied with relieving himself, he glanced over his shoulder, but he couldn't see anything. Feeling a little spooked, he quickly finished his bathroom break, zipped up, and prepared to walk back to camp— when he unmistakably felt a hand reach into his back pocket.

Spinning around to see what was happening, Paul got the fright of his life. There was a half-human, half-wolf creature standing on its hind legs, staring back at him with his wallet clutched in its human-like right hand. Now, most paranormal entities might not have much use for a man's wallet, but the Navajo tradition tells us that skinwalkers are actually human enchanters who can shift their shape. If that's true, this may well have been nothing more than a shiftless sorcerer looking for easy money to finance a night on the town!

In any event, whether you're a man or a wolfman, stealing is stealing. Paul didn't like being robbed, but as he looked into the face of this paranormal pickpocket, he didn't feel like pressing the point. And so, leaving his wallet in the skinwalker's grasp, he bolted back to camp, told his girlfriend to get in the truck with him, and sped down the road as fast as he could. He didn't have his driver's license anymore, but it didn't matter—at that point Paul would have been glad to be pulled over by a cop. He wasn't, but the next day his girlfriend suggested that he go to the police himself to report the incident. Paul was understandably hesitant; he assumed that he would be laughed at for reporting that he was mugged by a skinwalker. However, the officer who interviewed him immediately acknowledged that such incidents were not uncommon in the region.

Traditionally, though, the skinwalkers are better known as grave robbers than muggers. They have been responsible for many sleepless nights after Navajo burial ceremonies as worried relatives guard the tomb against them. It is said that skinwalkers try to dig up rings, bracelets, and other jewelry in order to gain power over the spirit of the deceased—not to mention the fact that they supposedly steal the very skin off the corpse so that they can try it on for themselves! (Hence the name skinwalkers.)

Certain other paranormal shapeshifters, however, have a longer history in the strong-arm robbery racket. It was way back in the autumn of 1913 that several residents of the Bronx complained that they had been mugged by werewolves. When police went to investigate, they found four strange men lurking in an alley. They gave chase on foot, but the four figures dispersed in four different directions. Nevertheless, one of the officers managed to get close enough to one of the suspects to try to slap the cuffs on him. But as he tried to do so, suddenly he was not wrestling with a human being but a giant wolf! When the horrid creature began viciously biting his leg, he was forced to drop the cuffs and grab his nightstick. He sent it crashing down on the beast's head, and whatever it was let go of him, ran down a back alley, and disappeared into the darkness.

So, is there truly a rash of skinwalker robberies taking place in the Southwest? How about a werewolf crime wave in New York City. Who really knows?

Duped by Demons

The comedic excuse "the devil made me do it" has been a running gag for decades, but is there any truth to it? Could the devil or his host of demonic minions really cause hapless human beings to commit crimes? Well, according to David Berkowitz, it's not only possible—it happened to him.

Berkowitz, better if less accurately known as the Son of Sam, became one of the world's most infamous serial killers in the world during the 1970s—on the orders, he says, of a demon-possessed dog owned by his neighbor Sam (the dog thus being the true son of Sam). All night long, Berkowitz would hear the demon dog barking commands to kill, demanding a blood sacrifice in the form of murdered New Yorkers. Whenever he left his apartment, its voice followed him telepathically.

So one Christmas Eve, while other New Yorkers were out shopping for presents, Berkowitz was out shopping for victims, guided by the voice of the demon dog in his head. And the dog was a picky shopper. Berkowitz noticed a few potential targets as he scanned the city streets. One of them was a slightly overweight middle-aged woman with her hands loaded with shopping bags. Out of shape and preoccupied as she was, Berkowitz reasoned that it would be relatively easy to subdue her and sacrifice her to Satan. But as he stepped toward her clutching his knife, the demonic voice in his head screamed, "No! Not her! Too old! Too old!"

The demon apparently wanted young blood, and when Berkowitz saw a young Hispanic woman walking over an isolated bridge, it cried out, "Her! She's the one! Get her! Get her!" Like a puppet, Berkowitz rushed up behind the lady and began stabbing her. According to him, he was just dutifully following instructions from his dark overlord. There was no malice on his part, and so he was a little surprised at his victim's strenuous objections to the exercise. Why was she struggling so much? Why was she so afraid? Why wasn't she glad to lay down her life for Satan? As a perplexed Berkowitz later told police detectives, "I wasn't going to rob or rape her; I just wanted to kill her."

The detectives exchanged glances. Was this guy for real? How did he *think* somebody was going to react if he went up and asked, "Excuse me, miss, I'm not going to rob or rape you, I just want to take your life. Is that okay? It's for Satan."? What, she was going to smile and say, "Sure thing, sir—go ahead and take a stab at it!"? The investigators quickly decided that Berkowitz was suffering from a severe disconnect with reality. A search of his shabby apartment, with its graffiti-covered walls full of antisocial messages of despair and isolation, only reinforced this conclusion

Of course, being a deranged psychopath is one thing; being bossed around by a demon is quite another. Was Berkowitz really taking his murderous marching orders from a demon dog called the Son of Sam? Who can know for sure? Berkowitz later recanted much of his story, and it's also unclear if his first victim ever actually existed. If she did, she never visited a hospital for her injuries, and if she died of them, her death went unreported. But one thing's for sure: Berkowitz would continue to follow the commands of the voice in his head—demon dog or otherwise— and would rack up half a dozen confirmed kills over the next few years after switching his murder weapon from a knife to a .44-caliber Bulldog revolver. Whatever inspired his crimes, they were absolutely despicable.

A more recent case of allegedly demon-driven murder occurred in 2016 when a North Carolina man named Jeffrey Ward killed his wife and stepdaughter. Ward admitted that he'd been arguing with the women, but claimed that as the altercation escalated he suddenly "blacked out" and was "overtaken by demons." The next thing he knew, he was standing over their dead bodies. Now, most people—and more importantly, most juries—might conclude that Ward was just flinging a load of BS to try to beat the murder charge. But that's not to say this defense never works.

All you have to do is look at the case of Michael Taylor, who killed his wife Christine in one of the most infamous murders of 1970s Britain. In the end, Taylor did indeed proclaim that the devil made him do it—but ironically, the roots of his reign of terror lay in a bible study class!

Taylor had recently started attending meetings of a local Pentecostal group called the Christian Fellowship Group. These meetings were led by a charismatic young woman named Marie Robinson, and while at first, Christine was supportive of her husband's interest in God, she soon began to suspect that he was even more interested in Marie. Taylor denied that but the more his wife bugged him about it the angrier he became.

Then one day, while in intense prayer with the Christian Fellowship Group, he completely snapped. But strangely, instead of taking his fury out on his accuser, he vented it on the prayer leader—Marie Robinson herself—charging at her with a demonical expression on his face as he screamed like an enraged wild animal. Fortunately for Marie, other congregants intervened and were able to restrain Taylor before he did any harm. Unfortunately for Christine (as it later developed), they didn't turn the crazed man over to the police; instead, they decided to pray for him. (They *were* a prayer group, after all!)

After a few preliminary prayers, they discerned that Taylor was possessed by demons, and then these dedicated Pentecostals *really* had to put their faith to the test by performing an impromptu exorcism. They found no fewer than 40 demons inhabiting Taylor's body, and to their credit, they managed to drive away 37 of them before getting tired and calling it a night. Figuring that the last three demons would keep until morning, they scheduled a follow-up appointment for the next day and told Taylor to go home and get some rest.

This proved to be a slight miscalculation, though, because as soon as Taylor *did* get home, he leapt upon Christine in full demonic fury. His first order of business was prying her eyeballs out with his fingers. He then began to tear the flesh off her face as the couple's pet dog frantically nipped at his heels. The loyal dog was too small to stop him, however, and soon became a victim itself when Taylor picked it up and proceeded to pull every single leg off its struggling body. He tossed its limbless torso to the ground next to his wife and left them both to bleed to death from their horrific injuries. He then ran outside, covered in their blood, and began shouting, "It's Satan's blood!" over and over at the top of his lungs.

It wasn't long, of course, before the police were called and Taylor was taken into custody. When asked to explain the terror he had wrought, he flatly informed the police that he had been "taken over by an evil force" which had ordered the slaying of "every living thing within the house." Sounds like another bogus insanity/devil-made-me-do-it defense, right? Well, if it was, it worked. Taylor never spent a day in prison for his gruesome crimes. Proclaimed legally insane, he was simply sent off to a mental hospital for a few years before being deemed to have been rehabilitated and sent back into society.

So sometimes the "demon defense" really does pay off. But is it always a sham? Or are there some cases in which demons really do dupe someone into committing wanton acts of brutality? Perhaps only God, the perpetrators, and the demons know for sure.

Catching a "Crime" Traveler

Since the late-19th-century publication of H.G. Wells' *The Time Machine*, time travel has been a bulwark of countless science fiction plots. But could it truly be possible? And if it *were* possible, just what would time travelers be up to? Would they just passively study the past, or would they actively try to change events in order to create a better future?

Or what if time travel were just a kind of amusement ride for wealthy tourists? In that case, there would undoubtedly be a whole protocol governing how these tourists would behave themselves. But as we all know, not all tourists follow the rules. Might some time traveling tourists break the rules badly enough to commit actual crimes?

Well, Dante Rashad Anderson, a 36-year-old man from Oklahoma (or from the future, if you believe his story) has claimed that he *wasn't* committing a crime when he stormed into an Arby's sandwich shop in April of 2016, shoved his way to the front of the line, jumped onto the counter, and demanded free food. The cashiers didn't see why they should give him any, so Anderson helpfully explained that where he was from—the year 2020—people don't pay for food; they just walk in and take it.

Now, that might sound feasible if Anderson were referring to cashless purchases made with an app such as Amazon Go. It's only 2019 as of this writing, and already there are Amazon Go stores where people just walk in with their phone in their pocket, grab stuff and go out the door, with the app automatically conducting a transaction between the store and their bank. But if that's what our hungry time traveler meant, he didn't say so. He didn't mention any app; he simply grabbed as many roast beef sandwiches as his time traveling hands could hold and began munching on a cheesy roast beef melt.

Seeing as he still had everyone's attention, Anderson then dropped another prophecy: "Oh yeah, in the future—in the year 2020—everyone on the planet is dead!" He didn't explain how *he* was alive if everyone from his time was dead, nor why dead people would need food, whether or not they paid for it. He just delivered the news of the upcoming extinction of the human race as a matter of record.

Well, we'll soon see if any of this time traveling roast beef sandwich thief's predictions come true. My money is on "no"— but if they don't, Anderson left himself an out. As he explained to the puzzled employees and customers at Arby's, we exist in a parallel universe separate from his, so what happened in his timeline may not necessarily occur in ours. Parallel universe?

Really? If you are feeling completely dumbfounded right now, just imagine how the people in this fast food restaurant felt! They might have been asked "Do you want fries with that?" before, but "Do you want a quantum physics lesson with that?" was pretty surely a new one.

The lecture ended abruptly when Anderson grabbed a bag full of sandwiches (and a handful of bacon for good measure) and made a hasty departure. Did he suddenly leap into a wormhole to go back to his own time, you might ask? No, this time traveling thief simply shoved people out of his way, burst through the doors, and ran out into the street while munching on a purloined piece of bacon. And jaywalking must not be a crime in 2020 either, because instead of waiting his turn at a crosswalk, Anderson just ran out in front of oncoming traffic. One motorist was barely able to brake in time to avoid hitting the bacon-munching bandit. Instead of being thankful, Anderson, as the driver described it, "leapt up like Chuck Norris" and began pummeling the side of the car with heavy, powerful kicks, putting big dents in the door with the full force of his body weight.

So what happened to our intrepid time traveler after he fled the scene for good? It remains a mystery... No, just kidding! There wasn't much mystery involved, actually; the police used security camera footage to identify Anderson and were soon knocking on his door. If he was from four years in the future, he certainly didn't look much different from the driver's license photo the cops had on file! He was arrested on charges of "robbery by force or fear, assault, and battery and destruction of property."

Sounds like he wasn't a real time traveler, right? Probably just a creep putting folks on. But interestingly enough, although he was laughed at all the way to the police station, Anderson stuck to his story. Even his official statement recorded in the police report about the incident is perfectly in character: "I am from planet

Earth and am four years advanced on you, and you guys are always trying to kill me. On my planet Earth, everyone is dead and I walked here from there." So Anderson is still claiming that he wandered over to our world as a refuge from a parallel universe in which everyone else on Earth was dead and it had become common place to ransack the abandoned fast food joints of the future for food. Does anyone buy it? Probably not... and we're probably all glad that run of the mill jerks like him can't really travel through time!

Or can they? Because Dante Anderson isn't the only boorish "crime traveler" to have been arrested in the last few years. Just a year after Anderson's Arby's raid, a man named Bryant Johnson was arrested for public intoxication after he was found standing in the middle of the street drunkenly shouting that he was a time traveler from the year 2048. So why had he come from the future? Just to get drunk and cause a ruckus? No, by his own account Johnson was here to warn us of an impending alien invasion. The strange thing is, the aliens that he wanted to warn us about were the very same ones that had sent him back through time in the first place.

And how did they do this, you might ask? Well, the arresting officers asked the same question, and slurring his words as they slapped the cuffs on him, Johnson happily explained it all. The ETs from the future had pumped him full of several bottles of hard liquor and then placed him on a giant pad. The pad had then sent some sort of energy wave through his body, triggering a reaction with the alcohol in his system and sending him hurtling back through time. Of course, an unfortunate side effect of the process was to turn Johnson into an incoherent, raving mad drunk. So, if those wily ETs wanted us to take humanity's harbinger of doom as a complete joke, well then—mission accomplished!

But there's at least one time traveling criminal who didn't end up in jail or the drunk tank, and he goes by the alias of James Richards. He was traveling through the desert desolation of the Southwest, watching for skinwalkers when he accidentally fell through some kind of wormhole. He emerged on the other side to find himself in a parallel universe, where he was rescued by a good Samaritan named Jonas. Jonas took Richards back to his home and introduced him to a brave new world where purple ketchup was all the rage and the Beatles were still on tour. (So were the Rolling Stones, but that's probably true in *every* universe!)

So what did Richards do with this amazing revelation? He pilfered a brand-new Beatles tape, of course, simultaneously abusing Jonas's hospitality and ignoring his warning not to take anything back with him for fear of disturbing the timeline that he came from. Yes, in this parallel universe they still use cassette tapes, and they apparently still make mix tapes, because what Richards got wasn't an official album, just a blank tape with copies of various songs. But he had Beatles music from another dimension in his thieving hands all the same.

Upon returning to our world in 2009, Richards converted the contents of the cassette to digital, created a blog, and uploaded the music for all to hear and judge for themselves. If you go to YouTube right now, you can find this supposed Beatles album under the heading *Everyday Chemistry*. Most who've heard it have two things to say about it: Number one, it sounds authentic; number two, that's because it's just a really good mix tape of Beatles solo material and outtakes all cleverly blended together.

Richards was ready for the critics, however. In one of his final online posts, he claimed that the reason the album has riffs and themes that we recognize to be from various Beatles solo albums is because that's simply our point of reference. But in an alternate reality in which the Beatles never broke up, the same thoughts, ideas, and guitar riffs manifested not in solo careers but in songs written together and performed by the full band. It is for this reason that we hear the same riff that Paul McCartney wrote for "Band on the Run" in our timeline in a Beatles song on Richards' stolen tape.

As hard as this tale is to believe, it's interesting to note that since the album was posted in 2009, no one has been able to prove that it's not new material. Not only that but after intensive searches from all corners of the internet, no one has been able to find out who this James Richards really is. But seriously, it's all just a bunch of rubbish, right? I'll let you decide!

Assaulted by Aliens

Much has been said, written and speculated about alleged aliens—and simply the very idea of aliens. Almost every single day NASA is announcing the discovery of a new exoplanet, and internet sleuths are continually planning to storm Area 51. But all across the board, space aliens are typically presented in a fairly sterile light. Sure, they snatch people up in the middle of the night and conduct experiments on them without their permission, but in most of the abduction accounts, the aliens display an even keeled, almost professional demeanor. Most abductees describe the ETs as behaving like a bunch of clinicians conducting research—no more and no less. They usually go out of their way to avoid inflicting any undue pain or discomfort, and many times they even reassure their captives that they won't be harmed and that everything will be alright.

But it seems that there are at least a few aliens out there that don't have such a good bedside manner. Some people have reported being roughed up in unprovoked attacks, as in the case of the famous Pascagoula Abduction. This event took place in the early 1970s and involved a young man named Calvin Parker and his older friend and coworker Charles Hickson. Although it has lost some currency now, the incident was well known for decades, and it still stands as one of the stronger claims of alien abduction because it involves not just one person but two people who have consistently corroborated the same exact story.

Charles passed away in 2011, and until he breathed his last, he maintained that the account they told was the absolute truth. With only Calvin remaining, most people figured that every detail of the story had already been told. But apparently, this wasn't the case. New information has leaked out, adding additional claims of criminal assault to an already sensational story. These new details came to light in 2019 when tapes surfaced from a hypnosis session that Calvin carried out with the late, great Bud Hopkins in 1993.

On the tapes, Calvin reveals some pretty nasty behavior by the ETs that accosted him and Charles. He describes how a female alien came into the room where he was being examined and took advantage of the fact that he was strapped to a table by smacking him around and even sticking her finger up his nose. He didn't get the feeling that this was part of the routine examination she was supposed to be performing; as he puts it on the tape, "She stuck her finger in my nose and she's got an attitude. She's got a bad attitude! Just as soon as I get loose, I'm fixing to twist her head off! A real serious attitude on that bitch."

It's clear from the tape that Calvin was filled with righteous indignation at this callous treatment and boiling over with rage. Soon, though, he experienced a different emotion: fear. Because he began to believe that the creature wasn't just toying with him—she was actively trying to kill him! At one point he got the impression that she was "changing his blood" as if it were motor oil, and as the process involved cutting open one of his veins and draining his blood out preparatory to replacing it with something else, he didn't seem likely to survive. Thinking that this was a kill or a be killed moment, as soon as the alien woman unstrapped him from the table he took the initiative and lunged at her, managing to wrap his hands around her "skinny little neck."

It remains unclear exactly what happened after that, but apparently, Calvin blacked out, and when he woke up he and his buddy Charles were back at the docks they'd been taken from. It was most certainly a rough ride for both men, and Calvin was just glad to have stepped off of it still in one piece.

Evicted by Elves

Elves are the tricksters of Irish folklore. They sometimes do good—but more often than not, they also do bad. Still, their crimes are typically fairly minor; they usually don't kill or seriously hurt anyone. According to legend and anecdotal reports, instead of doing any real harm, they delight in doing just enough to annoy the crap out of people.

The best response to elfish pranks seems to be simply to ignore them. Most of the time the elves get bored after a while and move on to bother someone else. And most people who have encountered them have adopted a policy of long-suffering good nature—both because it gets things over quicker and because the elves, while quick to find amusement in the foibles of humanity, are themselves are said to be very sensitive. And if ever they are provoked to genuine anger rather than just high-spirited mischief, the results can be downright horrific—for elves, despite their playful appearance, are said to wield enormous supernatural powers. It is for good reason that Irishmen always try to keep on the good side of the "wee people" they meet.

Sometimes, though, that's easier said than done, as was the case when James Johnson moved into County Mayo in the northwest of the Emerald Isle. James was a writer seeking the solitude of the Irish countryside when he rented out a quaint cottage at the end of a quiet little hamlet. For the most part, his neighbors stuck to themselves—but there were a few residents that he hadn't considered. A family of elves allegedly lived inside a giant boulder in his back yard. (In fairy lore it is quite common for these diminutive creatures to live in odd places like the sides of hills or even within large rocks.)

James's landlord had made a joking reference to this local legend, but James was not the type of person to entertain such tall tales. Nor was he the type of person to tolerate a big rock cluttering up his back yard. He promptly moved it to a less conspicuous location, but as soon as he did so, strange things began to happen. The cottage erupted in poltergeist-type activity, with doors opening and closing and lights flickering on and off by themselves. At first, James thought his house was haunted, which would have been frightening enough—but which could never have resulted in the bizarre confrontation which followed.

Early one morning, he was woken by a knock on his door. It was still a little before sunrise and fairly dark out, and James had no idea who might be disturbing him at such an hour. Half asleep, he opened the door. At first, he thought there was no one there, but then he slowly looked down and was shocked to see a trio of elfish figures standing on his doorstep. They couldn't have been more than two feet tall. His mouth dropped wide open as one of the little people demanded, "Why did you move our rock?"

James, suddenly beside himself with fear, tried to play innocent. "Huh? What rock?"

The elf, though, wasn't buying it. He made a kind of "humph!" sound, and after briefly chattering with his colleagues in a high-pitched, incomprehensible language, he turned back to James and announced ominously, "You'll be hearing from us!"

And after that the group just vanished—right there in front of him, they flat out vanished. Wiping his eyes, James tried to tell himself that he was still asleep—that he was sleepwalking and seeing stuff—but deep down he knew that he had just borne witness to something extraordinary. He was also highly intimidated by the implied threat, and he was not about to wait around for the promised paranormal house call. He swiftly packed up his things and moved out the next day... but in the back of his mind, he still fears that one day he'll receive another visit from his erstwhile elfish neighbors.

Menaced by Men in Black

The mysterious UFO inquisitors universally known as the Men in Black are indeed an unknown quantity. No one knows who they are or where they come from, but one thing is certain—they sure do seem to have an extreme interest in UFOs. Usually, this interest centers on silencing UFO witnesses, or at the very least keeping close track of their whereabouts. They lurk around in black cars, sometimes even black helicopters, keeping tabs on those who dared to make their experiences public. They seem hell-bent on keeping things quiet, but why, and for whom?

When the reports of these secret agents first came forth, it was generally assumed that they must be working for the U.S. government, whether the CIA, FBI, NSA, or military intelligence. The main question thus became why the government was trying so hard to keep a lid on UFO sightings, and this, in turn, led to the theory that the sightings were actually of top secret military aircraft which the government wanted to *keep* top secret. Adding fuel to this theory was the fact that some of the MIBs had flashed Air Force IDs.

But when the Air Force brass learned about this theory, they were so appalled that they sent out nationwide warnings that someone was going around impersonating Air Force officers! Besides being a federal crime, such impersonation was a grievous threat to national security, raising fears that agents of America's enemies might pose as military officials in order to gather intelligence for their Marxist masters. It simply could not be tolerated.

The Air Force's forthright rebuke to whoever was going around dressing in black and flashing Air Force identification cards made it clear that in at least some cases, the MIBs were not who they said they were. And many have now concluded that they are not from the U.S. government after all. As accounts of their strange mannerisms and activities have piled up, a new theory has emerged stating that they are not from *any* earthly government. The MIBs have a great preoccupation with UFOs and aliens, and in many ways, they seem alien themselves. Whether they are from another planet or another dimension, they do not act as if they are from this world.

Still, even if their origin is extraterrestrial, the threats the Men in Black make are very much felt here on Earth. Dr. Herbert Hopkins, a UFO researcher active during the 1970s, learned this first hand when he received a phone call from a man who wanted to talk about "flying saucers." Hopkins (not to be confused with the late Bud Hopkins) received calls like this all the time back then, and as he enjoyed the subject and had the rest of the evening free, he was glad to oblige this latest caller. He was in the middle of working on a landmark UFO case involving a man named David Stephens, who along with a friend of his had experienced a dramatic UFO encounter the previous year. Hopkins had already received several inquiries about the case from local journalists and UFO groups, and as the man on the phone claimed to be with the "New Jersey UFO Research Organization" he was all ears.

The man asked when he could come over, and Hopkins basically told him any time. The caller took him at his word in an almost unbelievable fashion, for it was less than a minute later that his doorbell rang and he opened the door to see a strange man dressed all in black standing there. There were no cellphones back then, and the nearest payphone was nearly a mile away, so it seemed impossible for the man to have gotten there that quickly. Nevertheless, Hopkins invited him inside and the two quickly got down to business about UFOs. At first, the man's questions were rather banal, but soon his line of inquiry became more menacing and he even suggested that Hopkins should "stop talking about UFOs."

Things got much stranger when the Man in Black started playing parlor tricks to prove his point. After announcing that Hopkins had only "two coins in his left pocket", he ordered him to take out the one that was a penny. The man was right: Hopkins did have two coins in his pocket, and one was indeed a penny. After Hopkins dutifully produced the penny, his visitor asked him to hold it up to the light. He then seemed to focus his concentration on the coin, and as he did so the penny began to shimmer in Hopkins' hand. Hopkins watched the coin shine a bright silver before turning blue—and then, to his astonishment, it became blurry and began to fade away before his eyes. He felt the weight of the penny fading as well, and the next thing he knew it had completely disappeared. As Hopkins gasped in amazement, the Man in Black made the bizarre proclamation that "nobody in this plane" of existence would ever see that penny again.

He then shifted gears once again by asking Hopkins if he was familiar with the case of Betty and Barney Hill. This was—and still is—one of the most infamous cases of alleged alien abduction, and Hopkins readily admitted that he was aware of the couple and their story. In fact, he had recently heard that Barney had passed away, and he mentioned as much to the MIB. The man replied with the odd remark that "Barney died because he didn't have a heart." Then, looking Hopkins right in the eye, he elaborated, "Just like you no longer have a coin, Barney no longer has a heart."

Now, in reality, Barney had passed away from a cerebral aneurism; his death had nothing at all to do with his heart. But having seen the coin's supernatural disappearance and now hearing this thinly veiled threat, Hopkins was deeply disturbed all the same. In fact, by this point in the discussion, he was so rattled that when the MIB again ordered him to "stop talking about UFOs" he was ready to comply without question. Even when the Man in Black demanded that he "destroy any information" he had gathered about his current case, Hopkins didn't hesitate. As this instance demonstrates, if the MIBs are guilty of any one paranormal crime, it's got to be witness tampering!

Drained by Vampiric Assailants

Of all the paranormal cast of characters to be found, you will probably find more people claiming to have encountered—if not actually be—a vampire, than any of the rest. Indeed, unlike Bigfoot, ET, and Swamp Thing—there are plenty of people out there who claim to be a vampire. In fact, whole underground clubs have sprung up in celebration of these supposed blood suckers.

But to be clear—claiming to be a vampire, and actually *being a vampire*, are much different. Anyone, after all, can drink blood, but by definition, a vampire is someone who actually *requires it*. A true vampire has no choice in the matter. It's not a fun game of role playing, or grown up pretend—it's a necessary way of life.

And if we are to believe that there are those among us who need to drain us of our vitality in order to survive—then certain vampiric crimes on the unwary are to be expected. As recently as 2011 a man named Lyle Monroe Bensley, who upon his arrest claimed to be a "500-year-old vampire from hell"—was charged and convicted of an outright vampiric assault.

Lyle Bensley had broken into a woman's apartment in Galveston, Texas with the apparent intent of drinking her blood. He wasn't there for robbery, rape, or murder—as is usually the case with such criminal break ins—nope, this miscreant made it very clear that it was nothing short of the blood in his victim's veins that he was after. Sneaking into her apartment, he crept up to her bed while she was sleeping with the intent of sinking his teeth right into her neck.

But when she woke up with a start, this would-be-vampire panicked and punched the young lady right in the face. As the woman tried to get away, he then cornered her in the hallway where he forced her against the wall and began to feed. Fortunately, this vampire's fangs couldn't get a good enough grip on the poor woman's neck, however, and she was able to break free.

Ripping herself away from the Vampire's hold, she raced down the hall and out of the apartment where she flagged down one of her neighbors. This neighbor turned good Samaritan took the woman into her car while her vampire attacker stumbled out into the parking lot. The blood sucking assailant then spotted them and with inhuman speed leapt at the vehicle.

Just like something out of a horror movie, the motorist slammed the car into reverse even as the blood sucker banged on the outside of the vehicle. Fortunately, the driver was able to hit the accelerator and drive to safety while the victim called the police.

The police arrived quickly before the vampire had a chance to flee the scene. He hadn't gone too far and was still on the apartment grounds "barring his fangs" and "hissing" at passerby while he cavorted around in nothing more than a pair of boxers.

Upon seeing this deranged individual, with guns drawn the police ordered him to stand down. But instead of complying this supposed vampire did indeed show some superhuman ability, supposedly running like an absolute madman at full speed, and scaling two high and imposing fences in the process. Despite these shows of incredible adrenaline, the police had effectively surrounded the complex, and were able to eventually cornered the blood sucker, and began to close in on his position.

As they neared, they could hear the perp howl and scream, and on more than one occasion he apparently cried out that he "didn't want to have to feed on humans." Apparently citing the aforementioned trait of a true vampire, this paranormal tinged criminal insisted that he was committing his crimes only out of necessity, not out of pleasure.

For most who witnessed this bizarre display the only thing that could explain its occurrence was maybe a bout of severe mental illness, drugs, or perhaps a combination of both. All the same, there were those on the force that were deeply disturbed by what they saw; with some veteran cops going on record to state that they had never seen "anything like this."

And the antics did not end once the assailant was in police custody and had allegedly been given time to "sober up." Because even behind bars he kept right on insisting that he was a 500-year-old vampire. He also insisted that he didn't "want to feed on humans" but he had no choice. He claimed that just as regular human beings need to eat food; he needed to consume blood.

He even pleaded with the guards to keep him under constant restraint "for their own protection" since he couldn't control himself when he "needed to feed." Upon officially being booked, according to police records on hand, this 500-year-old vampire was determined to be 19-year-old Lyle Bensley. With the vampire's identity uncovered, the police then set his bail for a whopping $40,000 dollars.

Bensley would lawyer up shortly thereafter and his lawyer would come up with a surprising defense. Apparently, Bensley had been to a party and drank some punch spiked with a powerful date rape drug. If this were the case, it makes one wonder why a drug that would normally knock someone out, would cause Bensley to have such a powerful burst of energy.

Nevertheless, it was later claimed that Bensely had completely blacked out after consuming the drug and did not remember any of his rampage from the previous night. Vampire or not, having complete amnesia of his misdeeds was rather convenient for this paranormal perp all the same. In the end, after it was all said and done, most would come to the conclusion that Lyle Bensley's claim of being a vampire is just about as bogus as a fake ID from 500 years ago.

But some of the accounts of supposed life draining vampires are much more stunning than Lyle's, and they don't involve any blood whatsoever. Because apparently, not all vampires drink our life blood so much as they drain our *life force*. There are actually quite a few strange accounts of folks supposedly encountering life draining vampires, and many of these alleged victims had no interest or knowledge of the paranormal before their fateful encounter.

This was precisely the case for Martin Martinez when he was attacked by a vampire in the early 1970's. His wife was out of town, so Martin was relegated to enjoying the evening alone with only a box of pizza and late-night TV to keep him company. Or at least so he thought. Because in the middle of his late-night pizza binge he was surprised to hear a knocking on his window.

Anyone who heard someone knocking on a window in the middle of the night would understandably be a little alarmed. But for Martin, it was even more peculiar because the window that was being knocked on was on the 2nd floor! Martin was startled but upon looking out the venetian blinds that covered his window, he saw nothing before him but the empty blackness of night.

Taking a breath, he reasoned with himself that he must have heard a bird flying into the glass. Even so, in the back of his mind, he knew that whatever wayward bird might have struck his window certainly sounded an awful lot like a hand knocking against the glass! Still—since this was the most reasonable thing he could think of, he just left it at that and tried his best to forget about it.

But a little while later when he finally turned in and went to bed, he heard a little more than a knock at his window—he heard a voice! As is often the case with the paranormal, it was right after he was about to drift off to sleep that he distinctly heard a woman's voice calling his name. Getting up out of bed he then proceeded to the same window he had checked just moments before, and once again looked out of the blinds.

To his surprise, he didn't see any birds flying around, but he did see the form of a woman floating before him. According to Martin, she was "clothed in shadow" but he could clearly see her face and as he looked upon her, the strange specter's visage broke into a big grin, as if happy to finally be acknowledged. But don't let the friendly façade of this vampiric assailant fool you.

Because upon gazing into the face of this entity, almost immediately Martin began to feel weak. It was as if his very life force was draining out of him as he locked eyes with this being. He began to outright "shiver with fear" as his body automatically went into full panic, even while his mind failed to understand. All the while the entity began to sing what Martin could only describe as an eerie "lullaby" that pierced right into his soul and seemed to put him in an almost trance like state.

In something akin to the sirens of Greek mythology, that led sailors to their deaths—Martin was literally becoming spellbound by this intruding, vampiric harpy's call. With the sound of her enchanted singing bouncing around in his mind, he felt like he was going under, and that soon he would be under this being's complete control. The next thing he knew was that he was reaching for the window and beginning to open it.
As he opened the window the floating vampire's tune became more and more intense. But then right as he was about to open the window up entirely, something "deep within" Martin screamed at him to close it. Utilizing some stored-up reserve of

willpower he didn't know that he had, Martin then reversed course and "slammed the window shut."

It was then that he seemed to have broken off not only the hypnotic-like state he had been put under but also the being's active draining of his energy. The vamp must have had her concentration disrupted by the loud, unexpected crash of the window, breaking her hold on her victim and allowing Martin to briefly recuperate. With his renewed strength he ran to the other side of the room and grabbed the one thing he thought might make a difference in this battle with darkness—a crucifix!

Yes, it is often a trope used in cheesy B-movies, but in Martin's case, it appeared to work because as soon as his vampire visitor saw it, she shrieked out in displeasure, turned her back, and vanished into the darkness from where she had come. Martin figured no one would believe him if he ever spoke of his bizarre encounter. But interestingly enough, when he finally broke down and told his wife about it, she seemed to have already suspected as much.

You see, according to Mrs. Martinez's own testimony, at the very moment that Martin was being visited by this life draining vampire, she claimed to have been overwhelmed with the feeling that her husband was being assailed by an "evil force." As a Christian, she only did what came naturally, she cried out to God for her husband's protection. Even while there are some people like Lyle Bensley who want to be blood sucking vampires; there are people like Martin and his wife who claim to have encountered real life draining Draculas' of a whole other order.

Conclusion
Making Sense of it All

Being the victim of a sudden, unprovoked crime is devastating. It takes you out of your everyday comfort zone and into a place of great danger. Thus one incident can transform a previously peaceful and idyllic world into one filled with fearful doubt and uncertainty. Suddenly homes don't feel safe, regular walks to the park do not seem routine, and a night out can become a nightmare. And these are the results of average crimes committed by average criminals. When you throw in the paranormal, things become well-nigh impossible to deal with. At least the victim of a conventional mugging can expect help from passersby and a sympathetic ear from the police. When you're burgled by a Bigfoot, about the best you can hope for is disbelieving laughter.

This book brings together some of the more incredible reports that combine the paranormal with the criminal. While some of these happenings may not qualify as crimes in the traditional sense, they serve to confirm the long-running theme of mischief running through all forms of the paranormal. It seems that most paranormal entities which interact with people have a strong tendency towards a "trickster" type mentality. In these cases, their primary goal is simply to stir up as much fear and confusion as possible—although the criminal results range from mere nuisance all the way up to murder.

From our perspective, it is very hard to make sense of these acts, but perhaps that's the whole point. Maybe a confused and befuddled humanity is the *intended* result when these paranormal perps come to play!

64

Further Readings

As we bring this book to a close, we would like to introduce you to some of the reading and reference materials that helped to make this publication possible. They all have various strengths and weaknesses as it pertains to the content of this book. But they all have merit as an extra source of information all the same.

The Truth Behind Men in Black. Jenny Randles
The Men in Black pose one of the greatest enigmas of the paranormal but this classic work by Jenny Randles does a good jump at laying out the facts as we know them so far. She goes through MIB encounters on a case by case basis, highlighting both similarities and disparities as she goes along. If you would like to get a better grasp on the phenomenon of MIB's this book provides an excellent baseline with which to start.

Close Encounters of the Fatal Kind. Nick Redfern
Ever since UFO researcher Hynek introduced his categories of alien contact ranging from close encounters of the first kind—a UFO sighting—all the way to close encounters of the third kind—contact with aliens, people have been trying to break down the exact dimensions of alien encounters based upon what occurs during the interaction.
In this book by Nick Redfern takes matters a bit further by describing what he has termed "Close Encounters of the Fatal Kind." In this category, Nick places encounters that were so traumatic for those who directly experienced them, that they did not walk away from them. If paranormal crime does exist, murder by visiting extraterrestrial would certainly be high on the list. Here Nick gives us an excellent overview of the possibility.

Paranormal Parasites: The Voracious Appetites of Soul Sucking Supernatural Entities. Nick Redfern

This is another good Nick Redfern book. This one goes through a whole slew of supposed "paranormal parasites" who enjoy stealing people's life force and—if they are not careful—their life itself. From shadow people to skin walkers this book details a wide variety of alleged parasites at work.

Otherworldly Encounters. Nick Slovik

Written by another Nick—this time researcher Nick Slovik; if you need a good compendium on otherworldly encounters this book has it. Just about all manner of strange entity is covered. From here you can glean many trespasses and even outright crimes that these bizarre otherworldly beings may have committed.

Passport to Magonia: On UFO's, Folklore, and Parallel Worlds. Jacques Vallee

Jacques Vallee has been a leader in the field of UFOs for quite some time. But what separates him from others is that he is willing to take a much different approach than his colleagues. For the most part, Vallee doesn't doubt that there is indeed something to the constant flow of UFO reports but unlike his colleagues he feels that these events are much more paranormal than extraterrestrial in nature.

Vallee does not feel that alleged spacecraft seen flying through our skies are necessarily nuts and bolts vehicles but rather metaphysical projects of the same variety of the fairy hill of old. Indeed, in Passport to Magonia, Jacques Vallee makes a strong case that the fairy lore of old and the UFO lore of today are one and the same. For Vallee, the trickster entity that plagued humanity as elves and gnomes have simply altered the lens through which we perceive them.

Since we are such a technology driven civilization, the elves are now presented as advanced technology-driven aliens. According to Vallee, despite the change in costume, their behavior—including the potential crimes they commit in their transgressions against humanity—are the same. This book gives a great perspective on how such mischievous entities operate.

Real Vampires, Night Stalkers & Creatures from the Darkside. Brad Steiger

The late great Brad Stieger was an expert on just about everything paranormal. But more than that he was an excellent investigative journalist who would go right to the source of a happening and gather as many first hand accounts from witnesses that he could. This book is full of the kind of riveting first hand testimony that makes Brad Steiger books so great. Here you will find tales about the Chupacabra, vampires, and werewolves—you don't have to believe them, but they provide excellent case studies for alleged paranormal crime all the same.

The World's Greatest UFO & Alien Encounters: Conspiracies, Abductions, and Little Green Men... Encounters Beyond Belief!

As the title just might suggest, this book provides a huge listing of all manner of strange encounters that have been reported over the years. Among them, you will find tales of the MIB, Chupacabra, reptilians, and the like. This book also highlights many obscure cases of alleged alien aggression such as cattle and even human mutilation cases. If you are looking for some source material about paranormal crimes, this book is a must have.

www.mysteriousuniverse.com

Mysterious Universe is always a great site to check out for the paranormal. Even though sometimes the stories can verge on tabloidesque kinds of stories, Mysterious Universe never fails to give detailed listings of all manner of alleged paranormal happenings.

Also by Conrad Bauer

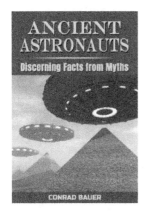

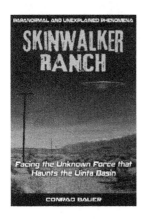

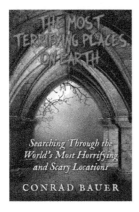
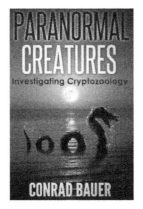

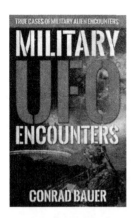